The White Cliffs

A Play

Bettine Manktelow

A SAMUEL FRENCH ACTING EDITION

SAMUEL FRENCH

FOUNDED 1830

SAMUELFRENCH-LONDON.CO.UK
SAMUELFRENCH.COM

FOR AMATEUR PRODUCTION ENQUIRIES

UNITED KINGDOM AND WORLD
EXCLUDING NORTH AMERICA
plays@SamuelFrench-London.co.uk
020 7255 4302/01

Each title is subject to availability from Samuel French,

depending upon country of performance.

THE WHITE CLIFFS

First presented at the Kilshawe Theatre, Deal, Kent, on the 19th September 2003 with the following cast:

Mrs Murdoch	Lynda Borley
Jane of "The Joysticks"	Gail Pointon
Joy of "The Joysticks"	Coralie Kavanagh
Gloria Glamour	Sophie Humphrey
Monty Marks	Peter Ryder
Serena Sartoni	Bettine Walters
Marvo the Magician	Pip Piacentino

Produced and directed by Bettine Walters

CHARACTERS

Mrs Margaret Murdoch, the landlady, fierce and domineering, 50ish

Jane, an attractive young singer and dancer, half of the double act "The Joysticks", late 20s

Joy, the other half of the act, brash and super-confident, 30ish

Gloria, the magician's assistant, pretty and naïve and a newcomer to showbusiness, 17

Monty Marks, a Jewish comedian, kind and warm-hearted, 50ish

Serena Sartoni, a singer with a superior attitude, 40–50

Marvo, the magician, a devious character, 20–30

The action of the play takes place in a bed-sitting-room in a boarding house in the Midlands

Time — Summer 1948

SYNOPSIS OF SCENES

ACT I

Scene 1	Monday morning
Scene 2	Thursday morning

ACT II

Scene 1	Friday morning
Scene 2	Sunday morning

Other plays by Bettine Manktelow
published by Samuel French Ltd

Curtain Call
Curtain Up on Murder
Death Walked In
Murder Weekend
Proscenophobia
They Call it Murder

ACT I
SCENE 1

A bed-sitting-room in "The White Cliffs", a boarding house in a Midlands industrial town. A summer morning. 1948

There is a window DL, *a door* UL *leading into the rest of the house and a door* R *leading into another bedroom. There is an armchair* DL *with an occasional table* US *of it. Against the back wall* L *is a small wardrobe. There is a divan settee against the back wall* C *with a small bedside cupboard beside it and another occasional table* DR *with three upright chairs around it. On the wall above the divan is a framed certificate for the Middleton Temperance Society*

The CURTAIN *rises. Mrs Murdoch, the landlady, enters followed by Joy and Jane, a singing duo, "The Joysticks", with their handbags and rather battered suitcases. Mrs Murdoch is a rather stern and domineering woman of around fifty, very much in charge; a lady of strong character. Joy is around thirty, a sophisticated, hard-boiled young woman who has been through the mill. Jane is an attractive woman in her late twenties; she is kind-hearted, ingratiating and rather too ready to please*

Mrs Murdoch This is it, first floor front, lovely view over the canal — but I advise you to keep the window closed at night.

Joy (*disparagingly*) Like that is it?

Mrs Murdoch Only in the summer.

Jane (*ingratiatingly*) Oh, don't worry about it. It's lovely, really! We've been in worse places — (*apologetically*) I mean worse *towns*.

Mrs Murdoch I hope you'll be comfortable. The settee makes up to a double bed. The bedding is stowed away underneath it. The small bedroom adjoins so I always let the two together at a reduced rent. That will be four pounds ten between you. Separately, of course, it would be two pounds ten each. I have to charge extra for baths, of course, because of the gas. One and six.

Jane That's fine, isn't it, Joy?

Joy (*looking round; disparagingly*) It'll do!

Mrs Murdoch (*indignantly*) It'll do!

Jane Joy didn't mean that. It's very nice, really, very nice!

Joy Very nice! (*She yawns and sits in the armchair* DL. *She looks glum during the following*)

Mrs Murdoch Yes, do sit down. Make yourself at home!

Jane (*apologetically*) We're both a bit jaded. We left London at five o'clock this morning and had to stand all the way!

Mrs Murdoch They're *our* railways now, aren't they? So they should improve. You'd think the war was still on.

Jane How true! Could I have a look at the other room, please?

Mrs Murdoch Of course. (*She opens the door* R) I don't usually let rooms on a weekly basis, you know; just bed and breakfast, for commercial travellers, itinerants. That suits me because it leaves the weekends free, but I heard at the theatre they were desperate for rooms so I said I'd take you for a week.

Jane (*looking into the room* R; *disappointedly*) It *is* small — very nice though, of course.

Mrs Murdoch I know it's small, but you have the convenience of having a sitting-room between you, so that's how I can reduce the rent.

Jane (*glancing at Joy*) Thank you very much. We're only here for a week anyway, and then we go to Blackpool for the summer season.

Mrs Murdoch That will be nice for you!

Joy We love Blackpool!

Mrs Murdoch You do look rather tired, I must say. Would you like a cup of tea?

Jane Yes, please. We have a band call this afternoon and then first house tonight.

Joy We should have come up yesterday but I hate travelling on Sunday. It's so boring.

Mrs Murdoch I can't say I approve of travelling on Sunday unless you absolutely have to. Some of your people did arrive yesterday, though. They said they wanted time to settle in.

Jane Oh, good, we're under one roof. That'll be nice!

Mrs Murdoch I shall come to see the show tomorrow. I advertise for the theatre so they let me have comps. It isn't really my cup of tea, Summer Revue, but obviously I'll use my complimentaries. What is it you do — in the show?

Jane Singing, dancing, a bit of comedy.

Mrs Murdoch Like a sister act?

Jane Sort of. We put the act together ourselves when we were in ENSA and then we thought we'd carry on after the war — just for a while.

Joy That's how it started.

Mrs Murdoch You must get on very well together.

Jane and Joy exchange a glance

Jane Most of the time.

Joy (*looking round disparagingly*) We have to — the way we live! In and out of a suitcase! Other people's houses!

Jane (*gushing*) Oh, but this is lovely! We thought so right away, didn't we, Joy? We were wondering about the name, "White Cliffs". I mean, it isn't near white cliffs, is it?

Mrs Murdoch It doesn't have to be, does it? There's a house further down the road called "Shangri-la" but it isn't in Tibet.

Jane (*with a forced laugh*) I never thought of that! Oh, quite! It doesn't have to be, does it?

Mrs Murdoch I lived in Dover all through the war; the front line, more or less. I wouldn't move until the war was over, it felt like desertion; but to me, the very name of "The White Cliffs" signifies our victory over the Germans. That's what kept them out — the white cliffs.

Joy You don't want to keep people out of a boarding house, do you, though?

Mrs Murdoch Figuratively speaking.

Joy (*sarcastically*) Ah, I see, figuratively speaking.

Jane (*covering up for Joy, quickly*) Who else is here? From our show, I mean?

Mrs Murdoch Monty Marks — he arrived yesterday. I've put him downstairs.

Joy Monty! Oh yes, he's Top of the Bill! We toured with him in ENSA. He's very funny.

Mrs Murdoch So I understand. He particularly asked for the ground floor because he told me he doesn't like stairs. Then I have Marvo the Magician in the back, with his young lady — she's *upstairs*, of course — and Serena Sartoni, Songstress Extraordinaire, she's opposite you. Very nice lady I thought, rather superior type — for a Summer Revue.

Joy Not like the rest of us — common!

Jane (*quickly*) So many of us all together, it will be fun!

Joy Yeah — great fun!

Mrs Murdoch I must tell you about the meals. I do like punctuality at meal-times. If you want breakfast you must be downstairs at nine o'clock sharp, no later. Lunch is at twelve noon and I would normally have the evening meal at six but as you have to be at the theatre by then I have arranged a meal for you at five o'clock. Will that be all right?

Jane Oh, thank you. First house is at six-thirty so that will be fine.

Mrs Murdoch Please let me know if you will not be in for any meals. You're paying for it, so of course it's your choice, but I do hate to waste food. Years of rationing have taught me that!

Jane You're so right!

Mrs Murdoch What is it you call yourselves?

Joy "The Joysticks". It's a play on my name.

Mrs Murdoch looks blank

(Adding helpfully) Joy. *(She picks up her handbag and takes her cigarettes and matches out of it. She gets ready to light up during the following)*

Mrs Murdoch *(not understanding)* I see. Well, I hope you'll be comfortable here. I do my best, though I run it entirely by myself — just with my son to do the handyman jobs. I'm a widow. *(To Joy, seeing what she is doing)* I don't allow smoking in the bedrooms — it makes the curtains smell!

Joy *(with ill grace)* Sorry! *(She puts the cigarettes away)*

Mrs Murdoch Yes, as I was saying … My husband died when my son was only six and I've brought him up single-handed since then, but he's been a great credit to me, my Danny. He went all through the war, the RAF, volunteered right at the beginning. "The First of the Few", Churchill called them. So many of them died, those young man, a whole generation. My son was fortunate enough to survive, although he was shot down twice. He was a hero.

Jane You must be very proud of him.

Mrs Murdoch I am. So — what was it *you* did in the war? ENSA, was it? That was entertaining the troops, I believe.

Jane Yes, that's right, Entertainments National Services Association. We were in North Africa and then Germany.

Joy We saw action!

Mrs Murdoch *(with a sharp look)* Mm, yes, that reminds me, I don't allow gentleman callers. It isn't that sort of establishment, not at all. I have my reputation to think of.

Joy Just give us a list.

Mrs Murdoch What?

Joy Just give us a list of the dos and don'ts, so we know what to do and what not to do.

Mrs Murdoch I don't keep a list, nothing like that! You have complete freedom to come and go as you please. I never lock the front door during the day, so you won't need a key. The only thing I do expect is that you be in by midnight. No respectable person would be out later, not even a theatrical person. Another thing, I do not allow drinking on the premises. I don't approve at all.

Joy *(pulling a face at Jane)* That's all right.

Jane We can't afford it anyway.

There is a tap at the door. Gloria enters. She is a pretty girl of seventeen, stage-struck, foolish and innocent but trying hard to be with-it

Gloria Oh, hallo — I thought I heard voices.

Mrs Murdoch Good-morning, dear. This is Mr Marvo's assistant. These two young ladies are also in your show — "The Joysticks". That's right, isn't it?

Joy That's right. I'm Joy and she's Jane.

Gloria I'm Gloria, Marvo's assistant. I'm on the top floor, all on my own.

Mrs Murdoch Are you quite comfortable?

Gloria Oh, yes, it's smashing! I love attics!

Mrs Murdoch (*looking pained*) I thought it would suit a young girl.

Gloria Of course it does. (*To Joy and Jane*) I saw your pictures outside the theatre, but I can still recognize you.

Jane (*with a laugh*) I suppose they *were* taken a few years ago.

Gloria I've been at the theatre all morning. Marvo's still there, perfecting a few more tricks before tonight.

Jane There's a band call this afternoon, isn't there?

Gloria Yeah, hardly gives us time to draw breath.

Mrs Murdoch I promised you a cup of tea, didn't I? It won't be a minute. (*She moves towards the door*) Oh, and I will need your ration books — pop them down on the way out, will you?

Jane Yes — we'll do that.

Mrs Murdoch It's terrible, isn't it, rationing! Three years after the war ended. The Germans are probably better off.

Jane I wouldn't be surprised.

Gloria I gave you my ration book, didn't I?

Mrs Murdoch Ah yes … (*Significantly*) The green one.

Joy and Jane exchange glances

Mrs Murdoch exits L

Gloria (*making sure Mrs Murdoch is out of earshot*) She didn't have to say that, did she, about my green ration book?

Jane You're under eighteen?

Gloria 'Fraid so! Don't tell Marvo, will you?

Joy How old does he think you are?

Gloria I told him I was nineteen. I don't think I'd have got the job if I told him the truth.

Jane Your secret is safe with us. Isn't it, Joy?

Joy 'Course — I always pretended I was older than I was at your age.

Jane Now you pretend you're younger than you are!

Joy Don't you?

Jane Natch!

Gloria Oh, I'm so glad you understand. (*She sits on the arm of the armchair*) I had such a job to convince my mother I'd be all right. I've never been away from home before. I wasn't even evacuated.

Jane Are you homesick?

Gloria Not so far. It's an adventure. But I am pleased you're here. It was rather lonely last night. It's such a funny old house, all twisty and turny with dark corners.

Jane Dark spidery corners!

Gloria I hope not. I hate spiders!

Joy So do we! You'd think being in the desert for nearly two years we'd be used to insects.

Gloria In the desert? What were you doing there?

Jane The eighth army mostly — at least Joy was.

Joy Shut up, you! (*To Gloria*) We were with ENSA, entertaining the troops.

Gloria That must have been smashing!

Joy (*sarcastically*) Yes, the war was certainly smashing — in more ways than one! (*She moves* US *and begins to unpack her case*)

Gloria My sister — now she was old enough to go out with the Yanks. She had a smashing time! So did my mum.

Joy Did their bit for Britain, no doubt!

Gloria (*earnestly*) Oh, yes, they both worked in munitions. Me — I was still at school, unfortunately.

Joy Never mind! You've got plenty of time to make up for it.

Gloria I've never lived in digs before. It does seem strange.

Joy I feel as if I've never lived anywhere but digs!

Jane Apart from this room all we've got is a cupboard! (*She indicates the door* R) Still it's only a week, and then we're off to Blackpool.

Gloria I am looking forward to Blackpool! We'll be there for the whole of August and Marvo says we're bound to play to full houses.

Joy (*stopping her unpacking momentarily*) How did you get tied up with Marvo?

Gloria (*moving* C) It was smashing! I answered an advert in *The Stage* just for fun. It said, "Magician's Assistant required. No experience necessary. Send a photograph". So I did and he picked me. He had ever so many answers, too, yet he picked me. I'm just amazed!

Joy I'm not.

Gloria All I'd ever done before was at Saturday morning dancing school. I mean, I haven't any *real* experience.

Joy (*with a sly look at Jane*) From what I've heard Marvo can teach you all you need to know! Theatrically speaking, of course.

Jane (*confidentially*) Look, dear, if you have any problems with him — any at all, just you come and tell us. Promise?

Gloria (*puzzled*) All right, but I can't see that I will have any problems. I don't know what you mean.

Joy Never mind.

Gloria I think it's all smashing! Just going in and out of the theatre gives me a thrill. It's so special, isn't it? I keep thinking to myself: "What would the girls back home think of me now?" I mean, they're all stuck in office jobs or shops or something else boring and I'm actually on the stage!

Joy Going places!

Gloria Yes, we really are going places. Marvo says the sky's the limit. He says we can get to the West End and tour Europe and go on cruise ships and go to America — oh, just about everything! I mean, we could be famous! Famous and rich! We could even go to Hollywood!

Joy Marvo has been shooting you a line! (*She continues unpacking, taking things to the wardrobe, during the following*)

Gloria What do you mean?

Jane She means he's exaggerating.

Gloria (*disappointed*) He said it *could* happen. I believe him. Why shouldn't it happen?

Jane Stage life isn't all glamour, dear. Most of it is just sheer hard work.

Joy And luck! With nothing much at the end of it. Not even a home.

Gloria (*crossly*) Well, I believe if you want a thing enough it will happen.

Joy You believe what you want. It's up to you.

Gloria (*offended*) Anyway, I'd better go and sort out my things. I didn't unpack yesterday. I was just too tired.

Gloria exits L *in a huff*

Joy The innocents abroad!

Jane I do hope she's all right. She's very young.

Joy She's not our responsibility.

Jane No, but I can remember when I was young and innocent.

Joy I try to forget!

Jane I can't believe *you* were ever innocent.

Joy Sometimes I can't believe I was ever *young*!

Jane Oh well, let's sort ourselves out. I'll have the cupboard. I don't mind, I could sleep on a clothes-line.

Jane exits through the door R *with her case*

Joy You might have to, after this.

Jane enters without the case

Jane In case you thought I was joking it really is a cupboard, not enough room to swing a cat.

Joy Good job we haven't got one, then. I'm not going to unpack any more. I've only got a few bits and pieces left. The costumes will be at the theatre. Oh, I'm right out of clothing coupons. Do you think we'll be able to buy some?

Jane We'll ask Monty. If anyone will know *he* will. (*She opens her suitcase*) There's no room for my clothes in that cupboard. I shall have to leave my things in here. I must have somewhere to put Tony's letters. (*She takes a small bundle of letters tied up with ribbon out of the suitcase*)

Joy You don't still sleep with them under your pillow, do you?

Jane Sometimes — but it doesn't help. I don't have nice dreams.

Joy Really you should burn them, Jane. It's not a bit of good hanging on to the past.

Jane No — I can't do that. I won't, not ever. I'll keep them until I'm a very old lady and then I'll show them to my granddaughter, if I ever have one!

Joy You and me both! Where do we ever meet an eligible man? I certainly wouldn't want to marry anyone in showbiz!

Jane No security!

Joy I can remember having stars in my eyes just like Gloria. After the war I thought we'd just go round the halls for a few months and then we'd get the Big Break.

Jane So did I! I had high hopes of the Windmill, say, or Victoria Palace.

Joy We're too old, dear, for the Windmill.

Jane Not for the stripping, silly, just to do our act. "The Joysticks": singing, dancing, a bit of comedy, a speciality act.

Joy Either that or I expected to meet Mr Right.

Jane Instead of which you kept meeting Mr Wrong!

Joy What about you?

Jane Oh, I've given up. I'll never meet another man like Tony. Everyone I meet I compare with him.

Joy (*sitting on the divan*) Pretty difficult competing with a dead hero! This divan — it's got no springs in it at all.

Jane You weren't expecting springs, were you? It must have seen some action.

Joy Doubtful with the old dragon at the door!

Jane If she wants to keep an eye on anyone it should be Marvo. I know him. I've played with him before.

Joy Figuratively speaking, I hope!

Jane Of course. (*She catches sight of the temperance certificate on the wall above the divan and bursts out laughing*) Oh, gosh — look at this! Mrs Murdoch is a member of the Middleton Temperance Society!

Joy She did say no drinking!

Jane Yes, but to see it on the wall — I ask you!

Mrs Murdoch enters L *carrying a tray with two teacups and saucers, a teapot and milk jug on it*

Jane and Joy both immediately stop laughing and look guilty

Mrs Murdoch I'm glad you're in such high spirits!

Jane Oh — just something we thought about — for our act.

Mrs Murdoch You do comedy as well?

Jane (*confusedly*) We do everything — really — or almost … I mean, nothing salacious — but just harmless family fun.

Mrs Murdoch I should hope so. (*She puts the tray down on the table by the armchair*) Do call if you want anything, won't you? Oh, did I tell you — there's a pay-phone down by the front door? It takes small currency up to a shilling. I don't allow incoming calls, of course, that would be too inconvenient. Do let me know if there's anything else you want.

Mrs Murdoch exits L

Jane Thank you — yes we will. (*She makes sure Mrs Murdoch has gone*) Oh, gosh, I do hope she didn't know what we were laughing at. Do you think she's charging us for the tea?

Joy Probably — if we've offended her! Anyway, what does it matter? It's only for a week.

Jane I do like to get on with people, you know I do.

Joy It's impossible to get on with everybody. You make yourself a doormat for people.

Jane (*indignantly*) I don't think I'm a doormat.

Monty enters L, *standing in the doorway*

Monty May I come in?

Jane Oh, Monty — lovely to see you. (*She moves to Monty and kisses him*)

Joy (*running to Monty*) Monty, darling! (*She flings her arms round him*)

Monty Don't suffocate me!

Jane Ignore her! She hasn't seen a man for two hours! Monty — you must come to my defence. Am I a doormat? Now be honest!

Monty If you are, you are definitely the nicest doormat I've ever come across.

Jane That's no answer.

Joy Jane is just being over-sensitive. Never mind that. Come over here Monty and look at this on the wall. We were just having a laugh about it when our landlady came in! (*She beckons Monty over to the certificate*)

Monty (*reading*) This is to testify that Mrs Margaret Murdoch is a Member of Middleton Temperance Society. *I* should have had this room.

Joy The landlady told us you couldn't manage the stairs.

Monty I can manage the stairs perfectly well *before* the show. It's afterwards I have the problem. (*He sits in the armchair* DL) So, she heard you laughing at her? Well, let's hope she has a sense of humour.

Joy She hasn't. No drinking, no smoking, and definitely no fun!

Monty That's what I thought. Never mind, it's only for a week. A good place for a tryout. I have the feeling that if you don't die here you won't die anywhere.

Joy Die — on stage, you mean?

Monty Where else? Have you see who else is here? Marvo for one! Have you seen his assistant? Lecherous lucky bugger!

Joy Jane is going to protect her.

Jane I'm going to try. (*She checks the teapot*) Sorry, Monty, there's no tea for you.

Monty Never touch the stuff. So how do you know the girl wants to be protected?

Jane She just seems so innocent to me, and I know what Marvo is like. I've come across him before.

Monty (*disparagingly*) So have I.

Jane What about the songstress? Serena something or other. Have you met her?

Monty No. I heard someone practising their scales at eight o'clock this morning. I suppose that was her. Woke me out of my beauty sleep.

Joy I just hope her repertoire is not limited to war-time songs, or we'll be in the soup!

Monty You still doing Vera Lynn?

Joy Of course — everything from *The White Cliffs of Dover* to *We'll Meet Again*!

Jane And I do *Lili Marlene* — à la Dietrich. (*She poses, hands on hips*)

Joy Then in the second half we do a medley from the First World War, *It's a Long Way to Tipperary* ... and of course the audience join in.

Joy ⎤ (*together, singing*) ⎡ It's a long way to Tipperary. It's a long way to
Jane ⎦   ⎣ go ...

Monty Nothing like originality.

Jane You're right there. Our act is nothing like originality.

Joy (*to Monty*) Gosh, you can talk! Most of your jokes I heard in ENSA.

Monty Most of them I got from ENSA.

Jane Funny looking back now those days seem so glamorous. I suppose we all had a heightened sense of reality, following the boys at the sharp end.

Monty Following the boys — it makes you sound like camp followers.

Joy We were in a way! I've never been so popular in my life!

Jane And you probably never will be again!

Joy Thanks a bundle!

There is a tap on the door L. Serena enters. She is aged between forty and fifty and is a singer; she is rather a prima donna and is a cut above the others in her own mind

Monty stands up

Serena Excuse me — is there another toilet? The one along the corridor is out of order.

Joy Oh, hallo — you must be our soprano.

Serena Serena Sartoni, Songstress Extraordinaire. (*She does a little bow*) I can sing through three octaves!

Jane We were wondering about your repertoire.

Serena I can't stop to tell you now — I'm just dying to go somewhere ...

Monty The bathroom is right at the end of the corridor and down a little step. But it smells terrible.

Serena Yes, she warned me, it's the old geyser.

Jane Don't say there's someone else staying here?

Serena No, the old gas geyser. Anyway, the toilet is out of order.

Monty There's one downstairs.

Serena Oh, thank you.

Monty Outside.

Serena Outside? Oh, hell!

Serena exits L

Jane She looks all right.

Joy What do you expect her to look like?

Jane *You* know. A prima donna.

Monty She's only second on the bill.

Joy Yeah — we know! Not like Monty Marks!

Monty Top of the bill. I've been there for years. Listen, I wanted to try my latest joke out on you.

Joy Must you?

Jane Go on — we're all ears!

Monty (*moving* C) I won't say I noticed. Here goes! "An old tramp knocks on a lady's door and when she answers he says he's starving and could she spare a bite to eat. 'Do you like cold rice pudding?' the lady asks. 'Yes missus,' sez he. 'Well, you'll have to wait a while,' sez she, 'because I've only just cooked it'." (*He laughs heartily*) What do you think?

Joy You wouldn't like to know!

Jane Really, Monty, that's not a new joke. It's an old joke ... You've been doing the same act for years. If you ever got on television you'd use up all your material in one night and never be able to do it again.

Monty Television doesn't interest me. It's a passing phase. They said movies would kill the theatre but they haven't and no more will television. People love the immediacy of the theatre. There's nothing quite like it. They love us — warts and all!

Jane I hope you're right, but I have a horrible feeling you're wrong. Theatres are closing all over the place.

Monty Legitimate theatre perhaps, but not concert halls, not variety. Radio has boosted us and television will too — you'll see. Besides, we can do stuff you can't do on television. Look at Max Miller — you couldn't see Max Miller on television.

Joy A bit too blue!

Monty And what about the nude shows and the gang shows — you can't see them on television.

Jane You don't really think variety can survive on nudes and blue jokes?

Monty Or jokes and blue nudes — depending on where you are!

Jane All right, blue nudes with goose pimples. *I* certainly wouldn't do it.

Joy (*disparagingly*) I don't suppose you'd be asked!

Jane Why not? You saucy monkey! I'm as good as you!

Monty (*placing himself between Joy and Jane*) You saying that has actually given me an idea.

Joy An original one, I hope.

Monty Something to spice up both our acts. What about you doing a couple of walk-ons for me? Add a touch of glamour.

Jane Dressed or undressed?

Monty Oh — almost dressed. I could do with some female help strutting around showing a bit of bum and bosom.

Joy Get one of the chorus girls to do it. We already have an act.

Monty We should be prepared to help one another! Being a stand-up comedian is no joke, if you'll excuse the pun!

Jane You're flattering us talking about glamour. You have to be eighteen to be glamorous in this business.

Joy You can't recapture youth — we lost ours in the war.

Monty That's not all you lost, by the sound of it!

Jane (*reprimandingly*) Now then Monty!

Mrs Murdoch exits L

Mrs Murdoch I am sorry about the toilet. I'll get my son to look at it. I had no idea it wasn't working. Miss Sartoni has just told me.

Jane Oh — it's all right.

Mrs Murdoch I do try to keep everything in working order.

Jane Yes, of course. Sorry to be a nuisance.

Mrs Murdoch And I meant to tell you about the geyser. I'm afraid it leaks a little bit. You should always keep the window open. I'll get it fixed before the winter.

Monty That's OK by me. I usually have a bath once a week whether I need it or not but I don't mind missing one.

Jane You speak for yourself.

Mrs Murdoch I did tell you it was extra, didn't I, for the bath?

Joy Yes, you did.

Serena appears in the doorway L

Serena That's better. I really had to run.

Mrs Murdoch I *am* sorry. I was just explaining. My son will see to the toilet. It's probably the ball-cock.
Serena Oh. Thank you.

Mrs Murdoch exits

Monty The ball-cock. There must be a joke there somewhere.
Jane Not one you could repeat.
Joy You found it, then — the outside lav.
Serena Yes, but I don't know how I'm going to manage in the dark. It's at the bottom of the garden and I'm afraid I have a weak bladder.
Monty I do hope you're not caught short in the middle of your act, dear — that could be embarrassing.
Serena (*moving to Monty*) I'm always all right on the stage; my main problem is at night.
Joy Perhaps she'll let you have a jerry.
Monty Now we're back to the war again.
Joy I mean jerry as in goes-under, not as in German.
Serena Oh dear, I wish I hadn't mentioned it now. It isn't the sort of thing you talk about, is it?
Joy An unseemly discussion!

Marvo appears in the doorway. He is aged between twenty and thirty and is a smart young man with an eye for the ladies

Marvo That sounds interesting. What is unseemly?
Jane Oh — Mike! (*She runs up to Marvo with a squeal and throws her arms round his neck*)
Marvo Put me down or I'll saw you in half!
Jane It's so nice to see an old face.
Marvo Not so much of the old!
Joy So this is Marvo — how do you do.
Marvo Very nicely, thank you.

Jane takes Marvo around the room and introduces him to the others during the following

Jane This the other half of my act, Joy, and this is Serena Sartoni, Songstress Extraordinaire — and of course you know Monty Marks.
Monty You had a different name when I met you before. Are you Marvo the Marvellous, or Marvo the Magnificent?
Marvo Neither. It's just Marvo the Magician.
Serena You open the show, don't you? After the chorus?

Marvo Yes, I excel at opening. If you can capture the audience right at the beginning, that's the real challenge — anyone can close it.
Monty I daresay you've closed a few in your time.
Marvo Not as many as *you* have.
Monty I see my fame is spreading!

Gloria enters L

Gloria Oh, Mike, I wondered where you were.
Marvo Gloria, come and meet the old pros ——
Joy Old pros! Thanks a bundle!
Jane We've met.
Marvo Isn't she pretty? (*He puts his arm round Gloria*)
Gloria (*giggling*) Oh — Mike! Don't mess about! I wanted to tell you something. When I was coming up the stairs ——
Monty When I was coming up the stairs I met a man who wasn't there. He wasn't there again today ——
Jane Oh, how I wish he'd go away!

Jane and Monty laugh — nobody else does

Marvo (*to Gloria*) Go on, darling!
Gloria (*glaring at Monty*) When I was coming up the stairs Mrs Murdoch was standing outside the bathroom so I couldn't pass her — and then she said a strange thing … (*She pauses for effect*)
Marvo We're dying of suspense.
Gloria She said her son was mending the cistern, only she closed the door so that I couldn't see him, and then she said "Don't be surprised if he avoids you, he doesn't like strangers." Isn't that odd? I mean, in a boarding-house how can you avoid meeting strangers?

Mrs Murdoch appears in the doorway

Jane (*seeing Mrs Murdoch*) Oh, Mrs Murdoch — do come in!
Gloria (*turning round with a guilty start*) Sorry, I didn't see you. I was just saying ——
Mrs Murdoch Yes, I heard you. I should explain. My son is very — shy. He doesn't like people, not since the war. He is a very private person.
Jane I'm sorry to hear that.
Mrs Murdoch (*to Jane*) Something happened — to his face. He's all right with people he knows. He doesn't like strangers. That shouldn't bother you. He keeps out of everyone's way. (*To the others*) You'll be pleased to know the toilet is working again. Please don't hesitate to report any more problems.

Mrs Murdoch exits L, *leaving the door ajar*

There is a pause. Everyone exchanges glances

Gloria I wish she hadn't heard that.
Jane It's too late now.
Gloria Why should he want to hide himself away? What can be wrong with him?
Jane His mother was telling us about him. He was a hero in the RAF.
Serena One of the casualties of war. Some of those who lived were as much a casualty as those who died.

Joy, Jane, Serena and Monty huddle DL

Joy It's all down to the war, isn't it? It changed all our lives.
Jane For better or worse.
Monty How could it be for better?
Jane The alternative was worse, that's what I mean.
Serena What terrible days they were! The doodlebugs, now they scared me most of all — just lying in bed waiting for the engine to stop, hoping the thing didn't land on you!
Jane We missed all of that — we were in the desert.
Joy Yes — we used to go to sleep to the sound of distant gun-fire.
Jane And sometimes not so distant.
Monty It's amazing — when you look back ——
Gloria (*explosively*) Oh, don't talk about the war. It's so boring!

Everyone turns and stares at Gloria

Joy Boring!
Monty For those of us who were in the thick of it, it was scarcely boring.
Gloria I mean talking about it is boring. After all, we all knew we'd win.
Jane Did we?

There is an awkward silence

Serena There were times at the beginning when we weren't at all sure we'd win.
Gloria (*trying to retrieve herself*) But what did it matter, really?

The rest of them are stunned

Serena Am I hearing correctly. "What did it matter", you said?

Gloria Yes — it just seemed such a waste when you look back.
Jane Waste of lives, certainly.
Gloria Waste of money, too.
Marvo (*making light of the situation*) Young people! They're all the same.
Gloria You don't have to defend me. I'm not stupid. I've thought about it, and I can't see what difference it would have made if the Germans *did* get here. We'd have survived.

There is a pause. Monty gives Gloria a hard look

Monty Excuse me!

Monty exits L

Jane I don't think you should have said that, Gloria.
Gloria Why not? It's history now, isn't it? That's what I mean about being boring.
Jane Monty is very sensitive about the war.
Gloria Why?
Serena (*severely*) It may seem boring to you, dear, but a lot of young men died so that you could have the freedom to say how boring you thought it was!
Gloria (*sulkily*) They shouldn't have been such fools.
Serena I beg your pardon.
Gloria Why go off and get killed? What was the point of it all?
Jane For us — for our freedom.
Gloria What does that mean? *My* brother had more sense.
Joy What do you mean, exactly?
Gloria He was called up like everyone else but when they were going to send him overseas he hit an officer and went AWOL. That sorted them out.
Jane So what happened to him?
Gloria He was caught and locked up for the duration, but at least he wasn't killed.

There is a shocked silence

Serena You admire that?
Gloria Of course, better a live coward than a dead hero!

There is an awkward pause

Marvo Yes, well, we've got a band call this afternoon, don't forget — better sort ourselves out. Come on — Gloria ——

Gloria Is there something wrong?
Marvo No, not at all!

Marvo smacks Gloria's bottom to move her through the door. She exits L

(*Turning to the others with a grimace*) See you later!

Marvo exits L

Serena What a silly girl!
Joy What a little madam!
Jane We have to forgive her her youth!
Serena Why? There were plenty of young men not much older than her who gave their lives for this country.
Joy She's just being silly, drawing attention to herself, that's all.
Jane She's in the right company. Marvo was a conchie!
Joy Gosh, no!
Jane Yes, he was. He boasted about it to me, that year in panto when you had the 'flu and I took a booking on my own. It really shocked me at the time.
Serena A conscientious objector! Prepared to let others fight for him! Deplorable!

Monty enters L

Monty Have they gone?
Jane They have.
Monty We must remember to avoid that subject, otherwise I might forget I'm a gentleman.
Serena *She* obviously didn't lose anyone in the war.
Jane *Most* people did.
Serena My husband died in Changi Jail, Singapore, 1943. Which is why I have to spend my time tatting around the variety halls to eke out a living. Nobody can live on a war widow's pension!
Monty (*sincerely*) That's a real shame.
Serena It is! That girl needs a good spanking!
Monty She certainly needs a history lesson!
Jane I do hope she doesn't say anything like that in front of our landlady. She told us her son was one of the "First of the Few."
Serena If I see him I shall make a point of being especially nice to him.
Joy We all will.
Serena Still, I'm glad the toilet has been repaired. I didn't fancy a trek down the garden in the middle of the night and meeting a strange young man, who doesn't like people, even if he was a hero.
Joy Never mind, dear, if you do come across him you can always scream for help in three octaves.

Jane stifles a laugh. Serena glares

CURTAIN

SCENE 2

The same. Three days later. Morning

The CURTAIN *rises. Joy's clothes are on the end of the divan and the bedclothes are rumpled*

Joy is standing by the window in her dressing-gown, smoking a cigarette. After a moment she extinguishes the cigarette

Jane enters L *with a cup of tea*

Jane Here — Joy, I pinched a cup of tea for you.

Joy Thanks, but I can't start the day without a gasper! She isn't around, is she?

Jane Too busy doing the washing-up. She's a real dragon in the morning, is our landlady. Breakfast is at nine o'clock and not a minute later. She starts clearing the table at quarter past! I had to go down this morning, I was so hungry. I didn't like to wake you, but at least I've sneaked you a cup of tea. It didn't go too badly, did it, last night?

Joy It's always better by mid-week. Nobody actually booed or threw rotten eggs.

Jane I can't help thinking, somehow, that there must be more to life than living in other people's houses, doing twice-nightly revue forever. I'd like to have a home of my own, sometime.

Joy You can dream, can't you? (*She sits in the armchair* DL)

Jane Oh — that reminds me about my dream last night. I was reading Tony's letters before I went to sleep and I had such an odd dream.

Joy I keep telling you not to read his letters ——

Jane I know. Anyway, last night it was more of a nightmare than a dream. We were back in the desert, you and I, there was bombardment in the distance, the way it used to be, booming all night long, flashing gun-fire in the sky … You know.

Joy Yeah — I got so used to it that when we came back I could hardly sleep without the noise of artillery in my ears. It was like a lullaby!

Jane In my dream, we were back there again, behind the lines. I was in our billet, on my own, lying down trying to sleep and I saw a young man coming towards me. He was in battle-dress and I thought it was Tony; I couldn't see his face, it was in darkness, but I called out his name. I felt happy that it was him, that I would see him again, because I thought I never would — but when he came up to me his face —— (*She shudders*)

Joy Well?

Jane Do you remember that time we came across a burned-out tank?

Joy Yes — after the Italians retreated. There was debris everywhere.

Jane Do you remember how we looked into the turret, not knowing there was anything, any*one*, inside? Just curious.

Joy I'll never forget it. (*She shudders*) We found ourselves looking at a blackened head. You could just about make out that it had once been a human being.

Jane That's what I saw in my dream. The face I saw.

Joy That *was* a nightmare!

Jane I woke up feeling scared. I just couldn't get to sleep again. You see, Joy, I never knew exactly how Tony died and I can't help wondering. I hope he didn't suffer — like that. (*She sits by the table*)

Joy Don't torture yourself.

Jane To be burned alive!

Joy (*sharply*) Stop thinking about it!

Jane I can't.

Joy And you should stop reading those letters.

Jane I can't do that either.

There is a knock at the door and Serena looks round it

Serena May I come in?

Jane Of course.

Serena (*coming in*) I managed to get down to breakfast. I must have my food.

Joy Jane brought me a cup of tea.

Serena I had such a disturbed night last night.

Joy You didn't have a nightmare, did you?

Serena No, it was Marvo and the girl arguing like mad right next door and then doors slamming. It was awful!

Jane I didn't hear them — did you, Joy?

Joy Not last night. Didn't hear a thing!

Serena I envy you. I'm a light sleeper and the racket woke me up.

Jane What were they arguing about?

Serena Oh, I couldn't hear any details, just raised voices, but I knew they were angry, both of them. At one time I thought I heard a slap — at least it sounded like a slap, a sharp cracking sound, and then it all went quiet. I was going to investigate but I thought it was none of my business. Besides, I don't like anyone seeing me without my make-up.

Jane I know what you mean.

Joy I wonder what that was all about.

Jane Lovers' tiff?

Serena Oh, you don't think so, do you? She's too young to be *involved* with him, surely?

Jane That's never worried Marvo before.

Serena I suppose we have to forgive her. (*She sits by the table with Jane*)

Joy For being young?

Serena For being tactless, dismissing the war as boring!

Joy Infuriating, I agree!

Jane Poor Monty. It was awful for him. His mother was a German and a lot of his relatives just disappeared in the war. He's never been able to trace them.

Serena I didn't know that — I didn't know he was German.

Jane Not really German. His mother was German-Jewish. His father was English.

Joy He knew so much about Germany that when we first met him we thought he was a spy.

Serena *Oh,* heavens! Did you really?

Jane But that seemed too absurd when we got to know him. It was too obvious! Everyone knows a spy has to be the least likely person, not the *most* likely.

Joy Except in a good spy novel when it would be the least likely person masquerading as the most likely.

Serena I think Marvo is a bit mysterious, but then I suppose a magician has to be.

Jane I know something else about him.

Serena Beside him being a conchie!

Jane Oh yes!

Serena Do tell!

Marvo enters L *in a panic*

Marvo Have you seen Gloria — any of you?

Serena Not since last night.

Jane What do you mean? She wasn't at breakfast.

Marvo Her bed hasn't been slept in.

Joy That's not unusual, is it?

Marvo She didn't sleep with *me* if that's what you mean?

Jane You're slipping.

Marvo This isn't a joke. She's disappeared. Her bed hasn't been slept in. The room is just as it was yesterday. She's just gone!

Joy Has she taken her clothes?

Marvo She must have. Her suitcase is missing.

Joy She's run away then.

Jane Why should she? (*Moving to Marvo*) Mike, what did you do to her?
Marvo I didn't *do* anything. We just had a bit of row.
Joy What about?
Marvo It doesn't matter what about. She went off to her bedroom in a sulk, and this morning she's gone. So what will I do now for a partner?
Serena You're surely worried about what has happened to her!
Marvo Of course I'm worried about what has happened to her, but the show must go on!
Joy Did she have any money?
Marvo Not much!

Monty enters L

Monty Why are you all so noisy first thing in the morning?
Jane It's half-past ten.
Monty That's what I said — first thing in the morning!
Jane You missed breakfast.
Monty Breakfast doesn't worry me. Sleep does!
Joy Gloria is missing.
Monty Missing?
Marvo She's not in her room.
Monty That doesn't mean she's missing. She could have gone for a walk.
Marvo She's not the type to go for a walk. You don't know her.
Joy Do *you?*
Marvo What do you mean?
Joy How well do you know her?
Marvo Well enough! Anyway, she could hardly have just gone for a walk with her suitcase. She's walked out, that's what, and left me in a hole.
Serena (*to Monty*) They had a row.
Marvo Only a bit of a row.
Serena I heard you shouting at one another.
Marvo (*sheepishly*) It was just a little disagreement.
Monty Enough to make her walk out on you.
Marvo Well, she shouldn't. We have a contract.
Monty You put her under contract?
Marvo A verbal one.
Monty A verbal one! Not worth the paper it's written on!
Marvo But what am I going to do? I must have a partner for my act tonight. (*To Jane and Joy*) Won't you help me out? One of you?
Jane Not me! I don't want to be sawn in half.
Marvo It doesn't hurt. It's a trick. Just come down to the theatre and I'll show you.
Serena Couldn't you get a chorus girl?

Marvo They're too stupid! Too young!

Jane I've never heard you complain about that before.

Marvo Oh, come on, one of you. Just help me out for tonight. She might come back tomorrow when she's calmed down.

Jane You do it, Joy.

Joy Why don't you?

Jane You'd be better — you're more adaptable than I am.

Marvo Go on!

Joy Oh, all right, but only as a temporary arrangement. I'm not going to do it indefinitely. You'll have to advertise for an assistant.

Monty She might come back.

Marvo Just until then — one way or the other.

Joy I'll expect to be paid.

Marvo I'll pay you a fiver.

Joy A tenner.

Marvo Seven pounds ten.

Joy A night?

Marvo Don't be daft! A week.

Joy All right then, a week or part of a week. I don't want the bother of learning it for nothing if she comes back.

Marvo You're a tough nut. All right, I agree.

Joy In front of witnesses.

Marvo In front of witnesses.

Serena (*rising*) I don't think I have the stomach for all this bargaining. Quite frankly it disgusts me. Anything could have happened to that poor girl and all you're thinking about is tonight's show.

Marvo It's important. Anyway, she shouldn't have walked out like that. She's a beginner. She can't afford to be temperamental. This is show business!

Serena Show business!

Serena stalks off L *in a huff*

Marvo What's wrong with *her*?

Joy She's a diva! I thought that all along. Now then, I suppose I'll have to rehearse.

Marvo Just a bit. An old trooper like you, you'll find it easy. Let's go down now for half an hour.

Joy OK — I'll just tart myself up a bit.

Marvo I'll get my things.

Marvo exits L

Jane (*to Joy*) That's handy! Another seven pounds ten a week. I'll bet you
hope the girl doesn't turn up.
Joy That depends how he treats me! Now, I must get dressed.
Monty Don't let me stop you!
Joy (*gathering her clothes together from the end of the divan*) I'll get dressed
in the bathroom. Thanks all the same!

Joy exits L

Monty It's a bit of a joke, really, isn't it, the magician's assistant actually
disappearing?
Jane I wonder what's happened to her.
Monty I'll tell you one thing — I didn't hear anyone leave the house after
midnight. My room is right by the front door and Madam locks and bolts
that door like a dungeon. I would have heard anyone opening it, and tap-
tapping down the path in high heels, I know I would.
Jane Monty! You wouldn't hear a thing once you got your head down.
Monty Normally, yes, but last night I was listening to boxing coming from
New York on the radio and I was wide awake. I tell you I didn't drop off
till well into the early hours and I'm sure nobody went out of that front door.
Jane She could have left once it was light. People are up and about here at
five o'clock in the morning. She could have caught an early train to
London. When you think about it that makes more sense than leaving at
midnight anyway!
Monty Yes, I suppose so.

There is a tap on the door L. Mrs Murdoch enters

Mrs Murdoch (*to Jane*) Excuse me. I have some change for you. You gave
me five pounds for the rent. (*She produces a ten shilling note and puts it
on the table*)
Jane Thank you.
Mrs Murdoch Mr Marks — I'm afraid you've missed breakfast.
Monty Oh, that's all right, I'll have a liquid lunch! I understand one of our
number is missing.
Mrs Murdoch The girl, you mean? Yes, Mr Marvo came down and asked
me whether I'd seen her. Of course I haven't.
Monty I was just saying I didn't hear her leave.
Mrs Murdoch She must have done. She isn't here, is she?
Monty Apparently not. Anyway, I'm off now. I have to see a man about a
dog. See you later!

Monty exits L

Jane 'Bye!
Mrs Murdoch (*looking round*) Are you on your own?
Jane Joy's getting dressed. She's agreed to help Marvo out — in place of Gloria.
Mrs Murdoch I must say it's very thoughtless of her to go off without a word to anyone.
Jane Apparently she had a row with Marvo. Serena heard them.
Mrs Murdoch Still — to clear off in the middle of the night! Where on earth did she think she was going?
Jane You do silly things when you're young.
Mrs Murdoch And say silly things!
Jane Yes, that's true.

Mrs Murdoch makes to leave

I want you to know how sorry we are about your son.
Mrs Murdoch Please don't feel awkward about the situation. He just likes to keep himself to himself. If you see him, don't feel you have to communicate. He would much rather you didn't.
Jane I'd like to talk to him.
Mrs Murdoch No, please don't. I know it's a funny thing to say but he really wouldn't appreciate it. He has absolutely no confidence in himself.
Jane If he mixed with other people he would have confidence. It would come back.
Mrs Murdoch I keep telling him that, but he doesn't believe me.
Jane I'm so sorry. Was it some form of shell-shock?
Mrs Murdoch No, nothing like that. (*Pause*) He was badly disfigured when his plane caught fire. It was over the English Channel. 1943. People used to watch dog-fights over Dover. I never could because I wasn't sure whether Danny would be in one of them. Sometimes we would see planes come down and pilots bale out, that sort of thing. People used to cheer when it was a German plane, a German pilot, but I couldn't bring myself to cheer. It was somebody's son, I used to think, or somebody's husband. But when Danny came down that last time it was night so nobody was watching. His plane was on fire and his face and hands were badly burned. He came down in the Channel. That probably saved his life. The sea was like balm to his burns. He floated around for what seemed hours, he told me, in his Mae West — you know, his life jacket — and then a patrol boat picked him up. He was in hospital for eighteen months, but when he came out — I'm afraid he wasn't like my Danny any more.
Jane I'm so sorry.
Mrs Murdoch (*wistfully*) You should have known him before the war, there was just nobody like him! Nobody at all! So full of fun he was, so popular!

My house was open to all his friends. Full of laughter and joy — that was my house! I liked them so much, those lovely young men! I made them welcome any time of the day or night. I'd make a meal, have them all sitting round the kitchen table, one big happy family. Many of them called me "ma" — just joking you know, but I loved it. What days! *(She sighs)* But now — so many of them dead, those young men, and those who came back, like Danny, were never the same.

Jane Just five years and how they've altered all our lives!

Mrs Murdoch So many lives ruined! When I think of my boy — the way he used to be! We had such a good relationship before the war. He was so much more to me than a son. He was my friend, my dear friend, my best friend.

Jane But surely — he still is.

Mrs Murdoch What? Oh, yes — of course — he still is. He always will be.

Mrs Murdoch gives Jane a brief smile and goes out L

Jane looks after Mrs Murdoch with a sad expression. Then she gets up and goes off R

The Lights dim then come up again to denote the passage of time to the evening

Joy enters L followed by Marvo. They are dressed for the show — Joy in her coat with a brief costume under it, and Marvo in a tuxedo. They have both been drinking. Joy switches on the light

Joy Shush! Jane's probably asleep.

Marvo I am shushing! Is she a light sleeper?

Joy Not particularly, but it's nearly midnight. We usually go to bed before this.

Marvo Let's just have another little drink, then I'll go, I promise. *(He brings a small whisky bottle out of his pocket)* A nightcap!

Joy You're getting as bad as Monty.

Marvo I'll never be as bad as Monty. Got any glasses?

Joy Here somewhere. *(She looks in the small cupboard by the divan and produces two glasses)* Do you think it went all right tonight?

Marvo Yes, you were OK. Just the right touch.

Joy That's your trouble — the right touch.

Marvo Oh, come on, don't be a meany! *(He takes the glasses and pours out two drinks)* Any dog is entitled to one bite!

Joy Yeah — only I'm not any bitch!

Marvo You don't fancy me?

Joy That's neither here nor there. This is a business relationship. It's the only way it'll work.

Marvo I think you should always mix business with pleasure.

Joy Is that what happened with Gloria?

Marvo Not at all. She was too young for me.

Joy I'm glad you realized it. What were you rowing about then — last night?

Marvo It was nothing.

Joy It was enough to make her run away, so it must have been something. She was so enthusiastic earlier in the week. You were going places — that's what you told her!

Marvo All I said was — (*with a phoney American accent*) "Stick with me, baby, we're going places!"

Joy That's not what she told us.

Marvo But I *am* going places — whoever is my assistant comes with me.

Joy Oh, yeah! That doesn't explain what the row was about.

Marvo If you must know it was over money.

Joy She wanted more?

Marvo Much more.

Joy For extra duties?

Marvo No, not for extra duties. I haven't reached the stage where I have to pay for it!

Joy Then what?

Marvo She seemed to think she was worth a lot more money than she was getting, that's all. I was paying her five quid a week and her lodgings. What more did she want? It's not as if I'm top of the bill.

Joy You're not even paying her Equity minimum for twice-nightly.

Marvo She's not in Equity — anyway, paying her lodgings makes up for that.

Joy You're not going to tell me what you get.

Marvo Probably more than you — but definitely less than Monty.

Joy He's top of the bill — you're not!

Marvo Oh, stop talking about money. I'll buy you a meal tomorrow and make up for it. Come here. (*He moves to kiss Joy*)

Joy You promised you wouldn't start anything!

Marvo I'm not! Just a kiss, that's all.

Joy Yeah, I know you won't do anything I don't want you to. I've heard it all before!

Marvo You pretend to be hard-boiled but I don't reckon you are underneath.

Joy You'll never know!

Marvo I was impressed with you tonight. I need a good partner. I'm fed up with these young girls just looking pretty and then bursting into tears if I criticise them. I could do with someone like you, a real trouper. We could really go somewhere.

Joy There you go again!

Marvo Well, you have to believe in yourself — no-one else will.

Joy I do believe in myself! I'm a "Joystick", along with Jane. I don't want a new act or a new partner.

Marvo (*grabbing Joy*) Couldn't I change your mind?

Joy Gosh, you're a fast worker! (*She ducks away from him*) Anyway, I'm dying to go somewhere.

Marvo That's a good excuse. Shall I wait?

Joy Suit yourself.

Joy exits L

Marvo pours himself another drink and lights a cigarette. His expression is optimistic. He hums a little tune to himself

Joy enters L

Joy I can't open the bathroom door — can you help?

Marvo What's wrong?

Joy It seems to be stuck and there's the most dreadful smell of gas, so for heaven's sake put that cigarette out.

Marvo (*quickly stubbing out his cigarette*) OK. I'll sort it out.

Joy and Marvo exit L

Marvo (*off*) It's not locked. There's something wedged against it. Give me a hand.

Joy (*off*) OK.

Marvo (*off*) Now — push together!

There is the sound of scuffling, off

Marvo (*off*) That's better ... There's something on the floor.

Joy (*off; coughing*) I can't see a thing!

Marvo (*off; urgently*) There's a gas leak! Don't put the light on!

Joy (*off*) I can't breathe.

Marvo (*off*) There's somebody here — on the floor ... A body.

Joy enters L, *stumbling and gasping for breath. She holds on to a chair. Jane enters* R. *She wears pyjamas and is rubbing her eyes*

Jane What is going on?

Joy (*still gasping*) Something terrible's happened.

Jane What? Tell me! What's the matter with you?
Joy (*coughing*) Can't ... Can't speak.

Marvo enters L, coughing

There's a body on the floor against the door — and there's the most terrible
smell of gas. Somebody call an ambulance.
Joy I'll go ...

Joy exits L, still coughing

Jane Who is it? Do you know?
Marvo No, and I don't know how bad the leak is. For all I know there could
be an explosion. Everybody must get out!
Jane (*moving towards the door R*) I must get dressed ——
Marvo (*grabbing Jane*) Don't do anything! There's a gas leak, I tell you.

*Marvo propels Jane out of the door L and can be heard banging on doors,
off*

(*Calling out*) Get up — get up, everybody! There's a gas leak. Get up! Get
up!

CURTAIN

ACT II
Scene 1

The same. The next day. Morning

The Curtain *rises*

Joy, dressed in casual clothes, is putting her bedclothes together on the divan

There is a tap at the door and Serena enters

Serena I wondered how you were — with neither of you coming down to breakfast today.

Joy I couldn't face it this morning. Neither could Jane. She's still asleep.

Serena I can always manage to eat. Sorry I couldn't smuggle two cups of tea up the stairs. Mrs Murdoch was busy clearing away by the time I'd finished. It doesn't matter that we went through a traumatic experience last night, rules are still rules.

Joy She is a bit regimental, isn't she?

Serena Hangover from the war. I wanted to ask you what you think is going to happen now. Do you think we can go on without Monty?

Joy I don't know. He *was* top of the bill. I suppose we could struggle through the rest of the week here but I don't know about Blackpool.

Serena They won't want us without him, will they? Marvo said he'd get in touch with them. He told me at breakfast.

Joy If they won't take us without Monty, that means we're out of work again.

Serena A dismal thought!

Joy It's a pig! (*She sits in the armchair* DL) Jane and I haven't got anything now till the panto. We'll have to go on the dole or do some factory work. What a bore!

Serena I'll have to get on to my agent, see what he can do. It really is a nuisance!

Jane enters sleepily R, *in her pyjamas*

What time is it?

Joy Oh, hallo, you're awake!

Serena It's nearly ten o'clock. You've missed breakfast.

Jane It doesn't matter. Is there any news about Monty?

Joy Nothing new.

Jane It seems so strange — only yesterday we were all laughing and joking together. Only yesterday! (*She sits behind the table* R)

Serena It's a warning to us. We should live every day as if it's our last.

Joy (*sharply*) What do you mean?

Serena Why you never know what's going to happen, do you? The girl disappearing like that and then Monty having this terrible accident.

Jane You don't think there's any connection, surely?

Serena There could be. I think there's a curse on this show. We aren't meant to do it.

Joy I don't believe in things like that, omens and such. That's pure superstition. All that happened is the girl decided to go home, for some reason or another, and Monty had an accident with the gas geyser. The two things aren't linked — why should they be?

Jane Exactly.

Serena But we still don't know what happened to her, do we? We don't know what happened to Gloria.

Jane We don't know that anything happened.

Joy Her parents promised they'd ring us if she turned up, and if she didn't they were going to inform the police. It's really nothing to do with us any more.

Serena (*stubbornly*) I still think it's an omen. (*She sits by the table* R)

Jane What about last night? I was so shocked when Joy came rushing in telling me to get up and then Marvo said there was a body against the bathroom door ...

Joy Sorry to be so dramatic but Marvo really thought the place was going up in smoke.

Jane *He* did all right for a conchie, didn't he? I mean, he didn't just save himself.

Joy He's not such a bad old stick. I'm beginning to change my mind about him.

Jane You do surprise me!

Joy I quite enjoyed it, being his assistant. It was quite restful just grinning inanely at the audience and handing him the odd rabbit in a hat. I didn't have to work half so hard as I do in *our* act.

Jane But surely there's much more prestige in *our* act?

Joy I don't know that I'm worried about that any more.

Jane And you actually like Marvo?

Joy I do — apart from having to fight him off in the wings! That's a bit tiresome!

Jane I told you he was like that.

Serena Weren't you going to tell us something about him yesterday?

Jane Oh yes, apart from him being a conchie — I know something else.

Serena Go on then ——
Jane He's married or at least he was the last time *I* met him.
Serena What and keeping it a secret?
Jane That's right.
Joy I don't believe you!
Jane Why not? It's true!
Joy I don't believe it. Or if it is true, he's separated or something. You know
  how difficult it is to get a divorce.
Jane You're not smitten, are you?
Joy (*rising angrily*) Of course not! Don't be stupid! It's just that I hate gossip.
Jane That's news to me! I thought you enjoyed it.
Joy It depends who it's about. I don't mind gossiping about other women.
Jane Just about other men!
Serena Mrs Murdoch would throw him out if she knew about him. She
  wouldn't approve of a married man masquerading as a bachelor.
Jane And she certainly wouldn't approve of a conchie!
Joy Well, he turned up trumps last night, didn't he? Getting us all out first
  and then going back for Monty — he probably saved Monty's life.
Jane I suppose he didn't give himself time to think.
Joy Why have you got a down on him?
Jane I haven't! I just miss Monty. He made me laugh!
Serena Everybody's miserable. The landlady had a face like a shovel this
  morning. She's bound to get into trouble over that geyser. She should have
  had it checked.
Joy I suppose so but we all knew the geyser leaked. She told us to keep the
  bathroom window open. Besides, Monty was drunk. I don't really see that
  it's *her* fault.
Jane This show has just been unlucky.
Serena It's cursed!
Joy (*sharply*) Serena, we've just said we don't believe in your stuff.

Marvo enters L

Marvo Why weren't you two at breakfast? Serena and I felt quite lonely.
Joy Couldn't face it!
Jane *I've* only just woken up.
Joy We were just talking about the show, wondering what will happen to us.
Marvo We'll be all right tonight. We can just extend our acts a bit, fill up the
  time.
Jane That's all very well for *this* week but what about Blackpool?
Marvo We'll have to manage without Monty. I've just rung the hospital. It
  isn't good news.
Serena There — what did I say? This show is cursed.

Joy Oh, Serena!

Jane (*rising; apprehensively*) Monty isn't … ?

Marvo He's in an oxygen tent. He's in a bad way.

Joy At least he's alive. So we'll have to forget Blackpool.

Marvo No, I don't think we should. It would be a tribute to Monty to go on. They still want us, with or without Monty. I've just put a call through to the management.

Jane (*moving to Marvo*) It wasn't your place to do that. Monty *was* the show. He's the only one with a name.

Marvo Are you suggesting *I* can't pull in the crowds?

Jane Yes, I am. None of us can, compared with Monty. We might as well admit it and give up.

Joy Well, I'm not giving up till I see Monty for myself. I'll go and visit him in the hospital, that's what I'll do.

Marvo (*quickly, putting Joy off*) They won't let you in. It's only relatives. The nurse said so on the phone.

Joy Did you say *you* were a relative?

Marvo No — they didn't ask, but they specifically said only relatives could visit.

Joy Well, I don't care what they said, I want to see him for myself. (*She picks up her handbag*) Who's coming with me? We can share a taxi.

Serena (*rising*) I'll come. It'll cheer him up.

Marvo I don't know about that.

Serena Do you mean it wouldn't cheer him up?

Marvo What I mean is you're wasting your time. I'm sure they won't let you in. He's in an oxygen tent.

Joy We can talk through it.

Serena Of course we can. I'll just get my handbag.

Serena exits L

Joy (*to Jane*) What about you?

Jane I'm not even dressed. No — you go. Tell me how he is. I might go this afternoon.

Marvo (*peevishly*) They won't let you in.

Joy (*looking in her handbag*) I must find some coins for the phone. Shall I give him your love?

Jane Of course. Say I hope to see him soon.

Joy I'll do that. (*To Marvo*) What about you?

Marvo Oh yes — give him my love, by all means!

Joy gives Marvo a mischievous smile and exits L

Joy Are you ready, Serena? I'll go down and order a taxi.

Jane I think you've offended Joy. (*She sits by the table*) You were a bit heartless talking about going on with the show when poor old Monty could ... Well, we don't know what might happen to him.

Marvo The show must go on!

Jane I wish people wouldn't say that.

Marvo It's true. Monty'd never cancel, even if somebody died, let alone if they just had an accident.

Jane It seems heartless to talk about it, that's all. No news about Gloria, I suppose?

Marvo If there was I'd tell you.

Jane I suppose no news is good news. You know, Monty said he never heard her leave the house.

Marvo At midnight Monty wouldn't hear anything.

Jane I suppose you're right. Monty told Jane he was listening to the radio. But she still hasn't turned up at home, has she?

Marvo Not as far as I know. She could be anywhere. She really isn't my responsibility.

Jane She is very young.

Marvo That's something she'll grow out of.

Jane Ha ha!

Marvo (*sitting at the table with Jane*) I don't see why I should be made to feel guilty about her. She chose to take off and she took off, and that's the end of it as far as I'm concerned. She let me down a stinker! (*Pause*) Has Joy said anything about going on with my act?

Jane (*uncertainly*) No.

Marvo Go on, you can't fool me!

Jane (*reluctantly*) Well — she did say you were a bit too handy! (*She demonstrates with her hands*)

Marvo Handy? Oh, I see what you mean. That's nonsense! I thought that was what she expected. You know how she flirts.

Jane Yes, she does, but she doesn't mean anything by it. It's got her into trouble before.

Marvo There you are then! Anyway, I thought she was very good last night, lent the act a bit of maturity. I might poach her from you.

Jane I wouldn't care. I could go solo — or else give it up altogether. It wouldn't break my heart.

Marvo Why's that? The glamour worn off, has it?

Jane Oh, the tinsel tarnished long ago. It isn't that. It's just that I can't *do* anything else and in any case showbiz spoils you for the more mundane life. No matter how bad it gets, you keep thinking the big break is just around the corner.

Marvo If you strike lucky!

Jane Ah, Lady Luck! This tour hasn't been very lucky, has it?

There is a tap at the door and Mrs Murdoch appears with two cups of tea on a tray

Marvo stands

Mrs Murdoch (*putting the tray on the table*) I thought you might like a cup of tea.
Marvo There you see — your luck's changed!
Jane (*surprised*) Oh, thank you. You are kind! I thought we were too late.
Mrs Murdoch You were, but I made a fresh one. After all we went through last night I thought that was the least I could do.
Marvo I'll leave you to it. I've got things to do.
Jane Oh yes, OK.
Marvo See you later.

Marvo exits

Jane This is kind of you! Only there's just me. Joy has gone to the hospital to see Monty. (*She sits down at the table and drinks her tea*)
Mrs Murdoch Yes, I know. She booked a taxi. I thought I'd join you in a cuppa, if you don't mind.
Jane Not at all.
Mrs Murdoch (*sitting down*) How *is* Mr Marks? Does anyone know?
Jane Marvo rang the hospital. Apparently Monty is in an oxygen tent. He *was* gassed, after all.
Mrs Murdoch I feel terrible about it. Although I did warn you about the geyser, didn't I? I can't understand how he came to pass out.
Jane He'd been drinking.
Mrs Murdoch That's what I thought. Dear me, it could have been a tragedy if someone hadn't found him.
Jane We're still not sure how bad he is. After all, they wouldn't keep him in an oxygen tent for nothing, would they?
Mrs Murdoch I was wondering what was going to happen to you. I mean, if he doesn't recover, it will ruin your show, won't it?
Jane They might try to get another comedian but I doubt whether they'd manage it in time for Blackpool, not someone of Monty's calibre anyway. He was — I mean is — very funny.
Mrs Murdoch Oh, I do wish I'd had that geyser checked before but I'm inclined to leave those sort of jobs to my son and he doesn't always feel up to it.
Jane Don't worry about it. Monty will be all right, I'm sure.
Mrs Murdoch I do hope so.

Jane How is your son?

Mrs Murdoch The same as ever.

Jane I thought we might have seen him last night with all that fuss and bother going on.

Mrs Murdoch No, he kept out of everyone's way. He didn't leave the house. He wasn't afraid. He never is. He's more afraid of ridicule than of any kind of danger.

Jane It's such a tragedy that he can't adapt to what's happened to him.

Mrs Murdoch (*after a moment, rising and moving* c) I thought he would at first, but when they took the bandages off the last time I knew it was hopeless.

Jane Were you there — when they took the bandages off?

Mrs Murdoch Yes, I was always there, sitting by his bedside. I only left him for meals. Whenever he had an operation I used to stay at the hospital and sleep in a chair. Anything to be near him.

Jane It must have been awful for you.

Mrs Murdoch No — no, it was awful for *him*. That day when I brought him home from hospital, he sat staring into space in utter despair for hours. He shut himself in his room, in the dark. He wouldn't let me in. I was patient. I used to leave his food by the door and go away. I wouldn't force myself upon him. Then after about a fortnight I heard him on the landing and I went up quickly. I begged him to speak to me. I followed him into his room and I sat at his feet and talked to him. I assured him over and over that I would always be there for him, that I would always look after him, no matter what happened.

Jane (*rising and moving to Mrs Murdoch*) Of course — you didn't care about his looks. Looks don't matter to a mother.

Mrs Murdoch (*in surprise*) His looks? (*As if recollecting something*) No, his looks didn't matter to me. My love was deeper than that, deeper than anything. But he knew that. He never doubted my love.

Jane You must have been a great help to him.

Mrs Murdoch (*facing Jane*) Oh, I tried, I tried so hard. But I soon realized that wasn't what he wanted. He didn't want the devotion of a mother, no matter how kind and well-meaning. What he wanted was the love of a wife, the love of a woman, and he felt that was something he would never know.

Jane He shouldn't think like that. It isn't true, anyway. You can love someone regardless of looks or disfigurement. Falling in love doesn't depend on looks. Otherwise half the human race would never experience it.

Mrs Murdoch I know that, my dear. I know it. But trying to convince Danny is a different matter. He *was* in love once, you see. He was engaged to a very nice girl during the war. They would have made a perfect couple. (*She moves* DL, *avoiding Jane*) But after the accident — I don't know what happened, we never heard from her again. She went away somewhere — married a Yank I wouldn't wonder. It broke his heart.

Jane Poor young man! I wish I could help.

Mrs Murdoch Nobody can help. It's too late.

Jane (*moving after Mrs Murdoch*) I can't believe it's too late. Why don't you let me see him? Speak to him?

Mrs Murdoch Oh, no — I told you, he avoids people. He doesn't like people.

Jane He's afraid of rejection, that's all. But I wouldn't be like that. There was a young man in the desert, Tony, I was — very fond of — and he was killed. There were so many things I would have liked to say to him, but I left it too late. I regretted that so much. I still do regret it. If I could help your son — I feel it would make up for that, for the fact that I couldn't help Tony. It would help me too.

Mrs Murdoch I suppose you're trying to be kind, but it wouldn't work. I know Danny. He wouldn't take the chance. He couldn't face rejection a second time. I know it.

Jane He's wrong — truly, I believe he's wrong. And you are too.

Mrs Murdoch (*indignantly*) I am!

Jane Yes, you are! You're too protective of him. You haven't given him the chance to face up to reality.

Mrs Murdoch What do you know? What do you know what I've had to do? Facing up to reality! What is the point of facing up to reality if reality is unbearable! (*She breaks away impatiently*) I must go out. I have shopping to do. You'll all be in to a meal tonight, I expect?

Jane Yes — I'm sure we will, except for Monty.

Mrs Murdoch moves away to the door L

I'm sorry if I offended you. I didn't mean to — I just wanted to help.

Mrs Murdoch I appreciate that — but the fact is you can't help. Nobody can.

Mrs Murdoch exits quickly L

Jane sits down at the table thoughtfully, her head in her hands

The front door slams

Jane rises, goes over to the window and looks out. She glances at her watch, then exits quickly through the door R

The Lights dim then come up again to denote the passage of time to the afternoon

Joy and Serena enter

Joy Discharging himself! That's Monty all over! Utter contempt for rules and regulations.
Serena And we've wasted the taxi fare! Five shillings between us.
Joy Marvo was telling lies, making out Monty was practically at death's door! That was wishful thinking on his part, if you ask me. He just wanted to take Monty's place on the bill.
Serena Oh, yes, I'm sure you're right there.
Joy I'd suspect he'd locked Monty in the bathroom deliberately, only I know he was with me.
Serena You *have* got a devious mind.
Joy Jane is always saying that. I wonder where she is, by the way. (*She looks through the door* L) Not here.
Serena She can't be far away — she left her handbag. She wouldn't go out without that, surely.
Joy Not very likely. I suppose now we will go to Blackpool, so we can be sure of another month's work.
Serena If Monty's up to it!
Joy Why else should he discharge himself?
Serena Perhaps he had a tip for the three-thirty!
Joy You're getting to know him well!

Jane enters L, *dressed in casual clothes and looking excited*

Jane I'm so glad you're back. I have something to tell you.
Joy We wondered where you were.
Jane I've been snooping — quite unashamedly. How's Monty, by the way?
Joy He's discharged himself.
Serena We had a wasted journey!
Jane What was all that nonsense about him knocking on death's door?
Joy That nonsense was Marvo speaking!
Jane So we will get to Blackpool after all. There was something I wanted to sort out before we left, something about this house.
Joy What have you been up to?
Jane Wait till I tell you. Is Mrs Murdoch still out, by the way? She went shopping.
Joy (*sitting by the table*) We haven't seen her. Why?
Jane I'll explain. I was alone with her after you left and she was talking about her son, and when she went out shopping I thought I'd just look around.

Serena sits in the armchair DR

Joy What a nosy-parker!

Jane I admit it, but it wasn't just curiosity. I wanted to find her son and talk to him. I just felt so sorry for him, and I thought if I could talk to him he might be able to see that there is another perspective to life. He doesn't have to shut himself away forever because of a disfigurement in the war. I thought I could help him.

Joy Oh, Saint Jane!

Jane Don't mock — I genuinely wanted to help him.

Serena Did you find him?

Jane No, that's the strange thing. I looked all over the house upstairs and down and I found no-one. You know none of the rooms are locked. I looked everywhere, but there was no sign of Danny.

Joy She said he never went out.

Jane That's the point. The only place I couldn't look was the cellar because the door was locked, but surely he wouldn't spend his time in the cellar!

Joy He might. It could be like a workshop.

Serena That's a possibility.

Jane Anyway, my courage failed me by then. I just didn't feel I could knock on a cellar door to see if anyone was there. It seemed such an odd thing to do. I suddenly felt rather nervous — afraid in a way.

Serena What of?

Jane I don't know. I felt uneasy. I felt — you'll think this is ridiculous, I know — but I felt as if someone was watching me.

Joy Where were you when we came in? We didn't see you.

Jane Ah yes, that's the interesting part. I thought I'd looked everywhere but I found a basement. Did you know there was a back staircase?

Joy No.

Jane It led to a downstairs room. I went down there.

Serena Why did you do that if you were already feeling nervous?

Jane I don't know ... I kept telling myself it was stupid to be nervous, and I just wanted to find out — to know.

Joy Curiosity killed the cat!

Jane I'm still here.

Serena Did you find anything?

Jane Yes.

There is a pause; Jane keeps silent for dramatic effect

Joy Well?

Jane It was a small room, like a den, or study, but with a bed in the corner. (*She pauses for effect*) It was definitely a young man's room. There were photographs all round the walls of school groups and groups of airmen. There were pictures of Spitfires and Hurricanes ——

Serena You did take a chance. Weren't you afraid he might come in?

Jane No, I didn't think about it. I was too engrossed. There was this photograph of a lovely young man in RAF uniform over the bed, but ... And this is the point, it had a border of black ribbon around it and underneath a little plaque which read "Per Ardua Ad Astra".

Joy The RAF motto. Something about the stars.

Jane That's right. I think it's "Through Struggle To The Stars", something like that. Then the dates: "1920 to 1945".

Serena Like a memorial.

Jane Exactly. If it were just for the war it should have read "1939 to 1945", but reading "1920 to 1945" it sounds like a life-time, doesn't it? Something that you read on tombstones.

Joy If it referred to him, to Danny, it would have made him twenty-five at the end of the war — about right.

Serena But what does it mean?

Jane I don't know.

Serena It could simply mean that the young man felt his life was over when the war finished.

Jane Yes, it could mean that ... On the other hand ...

Joy What?

Jane Nothing. I was pleased when I heard your voices, I must say. I simply flew out of that room.

Joy Why? What were you afraid of?

Jane I don't know. Only none of us have ever *seen* him, have we? We've never actually *seen* Danny. Perhaps we haven't seen him because he isn't there!

There is a pause while the three exchange glances

Oh, it's just too fanciful. Forget I said that!

Serena (*shivering*) Suddenly I had a creepy feeling. I don't know why!

Monty enters L

Monty Hallo, playmates!

Joy Oh, Monty, you did give us a scare!

Monty Don't look so dejected! I survived!

Joy (*going over to Monty*) You wretch, we came to visit you and you'd discharged yourself.

Monty Sorry I made such a rapid recovery. If I'd known you were coming I'd have lain there a bit longer.

Serena We're glad you're better, of course.

Monty Oh, thanks!

Jane I'm pleased to see you anyway ... (*She kisses Monty*) Are you better?

Monty Of course I am! The oxygen rejuvenated me. I feel as fit as a dog with two tails!

Joy Marvo said he'd rung the hospital and you were practically at death's door.

Monty The reports of my death were slightly exaggerated!

Jane But you shouldn't discharge yourself against the doctor's orders, that's silly!

Serena It's not as if it costs you anything now. It's all free! You should make the most of it.

Monty It was too boring. Besides I've got to make an urgent call to my bookmaker. Had a tip I couldn't miss.

Serena That's what we thought!

Joy Marvo *will* be surprised. I think he was counting on you not being able to do the Blackpool booking, let alone making it for tonight.

Serena That was just wishful thinking on his part.

Monty You'll be suggesting he tried to bump me off next.

Jane I don't think we could accuse him of that, but it was odd you should pass out so quickly. It was only a small gas leak! It's not as if you had your face stuck inside the geyser!

Monty I can't remember much about it. I knew there was a dreadful smell and I just couldn't open the door. The light didn't work. I suppose the bulb had gone and I couldn't see a thing.

Joy Just as well. Marvo said if we'd have turned the light on we might have had an explosion.

Monty How dramatic!

Serena You certainly seem all right now.

Monty I think the oxygen did me a world of good. (*He moves* DL) My brain feels really lively this morning. All the way back from the hospital I've been thinking up new jokes. What happened last night would make a good joke!

Jane Some joke!

Monty You shouldn't take life so seriously. It's much too short to be serious about it!

Marvo enters

Marvo Oh, this is where you've all gathered. Monty — you made a miraculous recovery! They told me it was touch and go!

Monty Yes, I'm afraid I'm back!

Marvo I'm delighted, of course.

Joy Don't try to kid us!

Marvo No honestly! I'd better ring Blackpool. They said they'd take us anyway but they will naturally be pleased to have you with us.

Monty *You've* been in touch with Blackpool! Taking over from me already!
Marvo Just helping out, old boy, no more than that. They're expecting us
for a band call first thing on Monday. We'll have to travel on Sunday.
Joy Ugh! Sunday travelling!
Serena I don't mind when we travel. I just don't want to stay in this house
a moment longer than I have to.
Marvo Why is that?
Jane It's a long story.
Marvo Tell me later. I'll get on to Blackpool and say it's all stations go! I'm
pleased, old boy, really I am!
Monty I believe you! Still *I'll* speak to Blackpool if you don't mind. I can't
be sure what you'll say.

Marvo and Monty exit L together, talking as they go

Serena That's good, girls! We have another month's work. I won't have to
ring my agent after all. At least this will see us through the summer and I
must say I won't be sorry to leave this house. I'll go and have a little rest
before the show. See you for dinner or supper or whatever she calls it.

Serena exits

Joy What a strange week this has been.
Jane I won't forget it in a hurry.
Joy I wish we knew what had happened to Gloria.
Jane I shouldn't worry. People disappear all the time. If they don't want to
be found why should they? P'raps she's run off to America to be a film star.
We'll hear about her one day in Hollywood denying she ever knew any of
us!
Joy I do hope you're right.

CURTAIN

SCENE 2

The same. Sunday morning

The CURTAIN *rises. Church bells are ringing in the distance*

The room looks as it did in ACT I, SCENE 1, *with all evidence of occupation
cleared away and everything looking neat and tidy*

*After a moment the door L opens and Mrs Murdoch enters followed by Jane.
Mrs Murdoch is in her Sunday best. Jane is dressed for travelling*

Mrs Murdoch You were lucky to find me in. I've just come back from church. I like the early service, so short and simple. What was it you left behind? I haven't found anything. Surely, you'll miss your train.

Jane It's a nuisance but I was at the station when I realized I'd forgotten something very important. I ran all the way back.

Mrs Murdoch I haven't found anything left behind. In any case you needn't have come back. I'd send it on — whatever it was.

Jane You didn't have a forwarding address.

Mrs Murdoch I knew where you were going in Blackpool. I would have sent it to the theatre. What was it anyway?

Jane (*moving to the door* R) In my room — under my pillow. You haven't stripped the bed yet?

Mrs Murdoch Not on a Sunday — of course not!

Jane exits R

Mrs Murdoch stands impatiently waiting with her arms folded

Jane enters R, *smiling, with her bundle of letters in her hand*

Jane They were under the pillow. That's where I always leave them. Letters from the young man I told you about.

Mrs Murdoch Something that precious — you should take more care of them!

Jane Yes, I know I should.

Mrs Murdoch You'd better hurry away now. I should hate you to miss your train.

Jane It doesn't matter as long as I'm there by tonight. Joy will sort out the digs.

Mrs Murdoch (*urging Jane*) Still — why hang about? You might as well go.

Jane Yes, of course. (*She goes towards the door*) There was something ——

Mrs Murdoch Yes?

Jane Something I should tell you. I feel a bit guilty about it.

Mrs Murdoch I can't think why.

Jane (*moving to Mrs Murdoch*) I'm afraid I did a bit of snooping before we left.

Mrs Murdoch (*warily*) What kind of snooping?

Jane I found that room — in the basement. I was looking for Danny.

Mrs Murdoch You shouldn't have done that.

Jane I didn't find him.

Mrs Murdoch Of course not.

Jane It's made me wonder. I've kept on wondering. You said he never went out and yet nobody ever saw him. I looked all over the house. I wanted so much to help him after all you'd told me. The only place I didn't look was the cellar.

Mrs Murdoch (*nervously*) There's only coal in the cellar — nothing to see.

Jane But I did find the den — in the basement.

Mrs Murdoch You have got a nerve, I must say.

Jane Yes, I suppose I have. But when I saw that room I'm afraid I jumped to entirely the wrong conclusion. You see, that photograph of Danny over the bed with a black border and the dates underneath seemed to me like a memorial to him and I thought he must be dead. (*She faces Mrs Murdoch*)

Mrs Murdoch (*aghast*) Dead! My Danny!

Jane Yes, I suspected you were keeping him alive in your mind but explaining his absence by the story about his face. I felt very sorry for you.

Mrs Murdoch You should save your pity for yourself! Look what happened to Pandora.

Jane There's something in that. But the box I opened revealed good not bad things. The truth for one.

Mrs Murdoch You think you know the truth?

Jane I do now. (*Pause*) I came back half an hour ago, Mrs Murdoch.

Mrs Murdoch (*moving* DR, *away from Jane; evasively*) Oh, I was at church. You must have had a wasted journey.

Jane I didn't. (*Moving to Mrs Murdoch*) Danny let me in.

Mrs Murdoch (*horrified*) He wouldn't do that!

Jane I must say it gave me a bit of a shock.

Mrs Murdoch Danny shuns people. He wouldn't let you in. This is nonsense!

Jane I should explain. I came back by design rather than accident. I deliberately left my letters behind to have an excuse, but the real reason I came back was that Danny left a note for me under my breakfast plate this morning asking me to, and suggesting I wait until you'd gone to church.

Mrs Murdoch (*astounded*) You're making this up! My Danny would never do such a thing! Leave a note for a girl — a stranger! Never! (*She heads for the door* L, *trying to escape*) It's a fabrication, a complete and utter lie!

Jane Wait — until you hear me out.

Mrs Murdoch stops

Danny saw me when I made my little recce the other day and perhaps he thought I looked sympathetic. Whatever the reason he decided to enlist my help — with a dilemma he was facing.

Mrs Murdoch This becomes more ridiculous by the minute.

Jane Believe it or not it's true. I have seen Danny. How else would I know about his face.

Mrs Murdoch His face! Ah, yes, his face!

Jane Why did you tell such lies, Mrs Murdoch? Why make your son out to be disfigured when he was not?

Mrs Murdoch There are all sort of scars, all sorts of disfigurements. His scars are on the inside. Nothing that shows.

Jane Nothing that shows, exactly. Danny is, in fact, very like you described him and exactly like his photograph, a good-looking young man.

Mrs Murdoch (*proudly*) Yes, he is that!

Jane So why the great elaborate lie about your poor disfigured son, so badly burned he cannot face the world?

Mrs Murdoch (*after a pause*) I don't expect you to understand. (*She moves* DS, *away from Jane*) His scars are on the *inside,* deep inside, in his mind. It's quite true what I said about him avoiding people, but his poor mind is crippled, not his body. People don't understand that I invented the story about his face to explain his behaviour. I was protecting him from their scorn.

Jane Your protection became a prison.

Mrs Murdoch A prison! Never! (*She moves to Jane, on the attack*) He would never say such a thing. You may have seen him but I don't believe he told you anything. You're making it up.

Jane Whether you believe it or not he wanted me to come back when you were out, so that he could talk to me. He has been a very unhappy young man shut up in his own mind, completely dominated by you. He longed to tell somebody about it, and he chose me.

Mrs Murdoch You're lying!

Jane No, why should I? (*Breaking away from Mrs Murdoch*) Much of what you told us was true, about him being a hero in the RAF and shot down several times. He was burned too, but he recovered. His face was unblemished. He kept going all through the war, recklessly he told me, feeling sure that every sortie would be his last. It was only afterwards when it was all over that he began to feel guilty about surviving when all his friends had died. He retreated from life, avoided people, wanted to hide. You could have helped him over that. (*She moves back to Mrs Murdoch* DL) But you, for your own reasons, encouraged him to shut himself away.

Mrs Murdoch What do you mean, my own reasons? Reason enough to protect him, isn't it? That's all I wanted to do, protect him!

Jane That's what *you* wanted, not what *he* wanted. The kindest thing a mother can do, Mrs Murdoch, is to let go, not hang on. You can't keep him a little boy forever.

Mrs Murdoch What do you know about it? *You* — a showgirl, not married, no better than you should be I shouldn't wonder, like all you theatrical people! What do you know about *me,* about my life? I've led a good, respectable life, with only one husband, one man ever. All these years I've been on my own and never looked at another man; something you people wouldn't understand.

Jane I understand enough to know you've been wrong — for a long time. Danny knows that too.

Mrs Murdoch (*furiously*) My Danny would never speak against me. You're lying to me! Get out! Get out of here or I'll throw you out bodily!

Jane Yes, I think perhaps you would. Only there's more you should know.

Mrs Murdoch I don't want to hear ──

Jane I know what happened to Gloria.

Mrs Murdoch (*evasively*) She went home.

Jane You know very well she never went home.

Mrs Murdoch She disappeared. People are disappearing all the time. In the war they used to disappear ─ bombed out, disappeared in the rubble. Nobody ever knew what happened to them.

Jane The war's over, Mrs Murdoch.

Mrs Murdoch (*speaking for the sake of it; nervously*) People said there were fewer murders in the war, but that's only because there were so many bodies. How could they prove if anyone was murdered or not?

Jane But we're not speaking about murder, are we, Mrs Murdoch?

Mrs Murdoch I thought... You're confusing me. I don't know what you're talking about, who you're talking about.

Jane Danny let me into the cellar. He remembered another girl in his life. A girl he wanted to marry. She just disappeared. Perhaps she was one of those bodies found on a bomb site. Who knows? (*She moves to the door and opens it during the following*) Anyway, he didn't want the same thing to happen to Gloria.

Gloria is revealed outside the door, supported by Monty. Gloria looks bedraggled and dishevelled

Mrs Murdoch reacts with dismay. Monty and Gloria look at her accusingly

Jane Monty came back with me just now. I was glad of that.

Mrs Murdoch That girl! (*She points a finger at Gloria*)

Gloria Look at what you did to me! Look at me! Danny saved me. Your son saved me. You meant to kill me!

Mrs Murdoch No, no, never. (*Moving* R, *in some panic*) It was a mistake. I wouldn't hurt anybody, not ever!

Monty (*to Jane*) I've called a taxi. I think she'll be all right as soon as she's fed and watered.

Gloria No thanks to *her*. If it hadn't been for her son I'd be dead. She locked me in the cellar. She'd have left me there to starve. Just because I laughed at her, her and her silly make-believe!

Mrs Murdoch (*addressing the others*) She doesn't know what she's talking about. The stupid girl! You can't believe her, surely!

Gloria I saw her son that night when I went down there. I wanted a key to my room to shut Marvo out and I *saw* her son.

Jane Yes, I know what you mean. I've seen him too.

Gloria Pretending he was something out of a horror story, when he was nothing like that. I laughed. Of course I laughed. And *she* hit me! She hit me so hard I passed out and when I came to I was locked in the cellar — in the dark, alone and with my hands tied ...

Mrs Murdoch Nonsense, nonsense! You surely don't believe all this.

Gloria She tied me up — look at my wrists, they're still sore. She shut me up in the cellar in the dark with spiders and all sorts of horrible things! I was so cold and hungry! How could she do it? I feel so awful, so weak ...

Monty (*leading Gloria to the armchair and sitting her in it*) Sit down a minute. The taxi will be here soon and then we'll go ...

Gloria I just can't understand why she did such an awful thing to me. I've never hurt her.

Mrs Murdoch I don't know what she's talking about. I don't admit a thing, but whatever happened it doesn't seem to have done her much harm. You didn't find it boring, did you, girl?

Gloria Boring!

Monty I think I know what you mean, Mrs Murdoch. You were teaching Gloria a lesson. Bit drastic though, wasn't it?

Gloria I don't understand. What does she mean?

Jane Don't you remember saying it was boring talking about the war?

Gloria Oh, heavens, I didn't mean it. She didn't have to go potty, did she, and lock me in the cellar? I shall never forgive her. In the dark and with hardly anything to eat or drink for three days! If it hadn't been for Danny *she* would have let me starve.

Mrs Murdoch I never would! Don't talk nonsense!

Gloria You all go on about the war as if no-one else suffered. I had to be dug out of a bombed house when I was a little girl! Dug out — do you hear? And then she did that to me! It brought it all back. I was so frightened! (*She sobs*)

Jane (*sitting on the arm of the armchair*) Poor girl! If only we'd known. If only we'd searched the cellar!

Monty I had my suspicions. I think that's why I had that little accident in the bathroom.

Mrs Murdoch No, you're wrong. I would never hurt anyone. I never *meant* to hurt anyone.

Jane I think you did. In order to bind your son to you, you'd resort to anything. But you might as well face up to it. It's over. Danny is free at last!

Mrs Murdoch Why do you say that? Free? Why should Danny want to be free? He needs me. I am his anchor, his roots. Once you've gone everything will be the same as it's ever been — just Danny and me and our occasional nice gentleman guests, not theatricals, not snoopers, not hysterical little exhibitionists, just normal people!

Monty You don't seriously believe you are going to get away with all this and go back to the way your life was before?

Mrs Murdoch Of course — there's no harm done, not at all.
Jane What about Gloria? You locked her up against her will.
Mrs Murdoch I haven't admitted anything. Besides it's done her no harm. Taught her a lesson. that's all! Character-building they called it in my day, a bit of hardship.
Jane A bit of hardship? Locked up for three days. Rather more than a bit of hardship! So, Gloria, what are you going to do? Shall we go to the police?
Gloria No, I just want to go home. I want to go home to my mum. (*She gives a little sob*) I don't want to go to the police and I don't want to be on the stage. I don't care about showbusiness any more; I just want to go home.
Monty You're lucky, Mrs Murdoch. Young Gloria is not as vindictive as you are!
Jane (*putting an arm round Gloria*) All right, dear, we respect your wishes. We'll see that you get home safely.
Mrs Murdoch That's right, go! And good riddance to you. Leave me alone with my Danny. We don't need anybody else.
Jane You will be alone, Mrs Murdoch, but not with Danny.
Mrs Murdoch What do you mean?

There is a knock on the door downstairs

Jane That must be our taxi. Is Gloria's luggage by the door?
Monty Yes, I saw to that.
Gloria Am I really going home at last? I just want to go home.
Monty Yes, yes, you can go home. We'll tidy you up and put you on a Pullman and you can have a slap-up breakfast on the way.

Monty helps Gloria to the door during the following

Gloria Thank you, Monty. I've had enough of showbusiness to last me a lifetime. I just want to go home!
Monty (*to Jane*) Are you coming?
Jane Yes — I won't be a minute.

Monty and Gloria exit L

Jane (*moving to Mrs Murdoch*) I'm sorry to be the one to tell you, Mrs Murdoch, but Danny is leaving you. He's quite resolved. He's coming with us.
Mrs Murdoch With you? Oh, never! I've brought him up to be a decent young man. He wouldn't have anything to do with theatrical people. Why should he go with you?
Jane Because he has nowhere else to go, and because we've asked him. Monty said he'd find him a job backstage. He'll need help. It will be hard for him initially adjusting to life outside of prison.
Mrs Murdoch Prison? How dare you? You bitch!

Jane Wasn't it prison? The worst kind of prison — an emotional one. He's longed to leave you, Mrs Murdoch, for years. He just needed someone to give him a gentle push.

Mrs Murdoch And you did that, did you? Gave him a push?

Jane I simply pointed him in the right direction — to the door. He's leaving you now and if you're sensible you won't try to stop him. After all, Gloria might decide to go to the police.

Mrs Murdoch Blackmail now! That's it, is it? That's the sort of person you are!

Jane I'm a determined sort of person, Mrs Murdoch, that's all! I'd better go. Danny is waiting for me.

Mrs Murdoch Waiting for *you*. Never! Oh, you vixen, you devil!

Jane Yes, Mrs Murdoch, I like you too!

Jane exits

Mrs Murdoch (*whispering*) He won't leave me. He won't! He can't! Not my Danny! (*She moves slowly to the window and looks out*)

The door slams downstairs

(*A desperate shriek*) No!

CURTAIN

FURNITURE AND PROPERTY LIST

ACT I
SCENE 1

On stage: Armchair
Small wardrobe
Divan settee
Small bedside cupboard. *In it*: two glasses
Occasional table with three upright chairs around it
Framed certificate for Middleton Temperance Society
Ashtrays

Off stage: Handbags and rather battered suitcases (**Joy** and **Jane**). *In* **Joy**'*s handbag*: cigarettes, matches. *In her suitcase*: Joy's clothes etc. *In Jane's suitcase*: small bundle of letters tied up with ribbon
Tray with two teacups and saucers (tea already poured) , teapot, milk jug (**Mrs Murdoch**)

SCENE 2

Strike: Tray with tea things

Set: Items of **Joy**'s clothing on divan. Bedclothes rumpled
Cigarette for **Joy**

Off stage: Cup of tea (**Jane**)

Personal: Ten shilling note (**Mrs Murdoch**)
Bottle of whisky, cigarettes and matches (**Marvo**)

ACT II
SCENE 1

Strike: Whisky bottle and glasses
Joy's clothes
Teacup and saucer

Set: **Joy**'s handbag

Off stage: Two cups of tea on a tray (**Mrs Murdoch**)

During lighting change p. 37

Strike: Tea tray and cups

SCENE 2

Strike: All **Joy**'s possessions

Re-set: Tidy room and make bed neatly

LIGHTING PLOT

Practical fittings required: nil
One interior with corridor, bedroom and window backings

ACT I, Scene 1

To open: General interior and exterior lighting; summer morning effect

No cues

ACT I, Scene 2

To open: General interior and exterior lighting; summer morning effect

Cue 1 **Jane** goes off R   (Page 25)
          Dim lights; pause; bring up evening setting
              on exterior backing and corridor backing

Cue 2 **Joy** switches on the light   (Page 25)
          Bring up interior lights

ACT II, Scene 1

To open: General interior and exterior lighting; summer morning effect

Cue 3 **Jane** exits R   (Page 36)
          Dim lights; pause; bring up afternoon setting

ACT II, Scene 2

To open: General interior and exterior lighting; summer morning effect

No cues

EFFECTS PLOT

ACT I

No cues

ACT II

Cue 1   **Jane** sits at the table, her head in her hands   (Page 36)
Front door slams

Cue 2   **Mrs Murdoch**: "What do you mean?"   (Page 47)
Knock on door downstairs

Cue 3   **Mrs Murdoch** moves slowly to the window and looks out (Page 48)
Door slams downstairs

THE WHITE CLIFFS by Bettine Manktelow

A number of printing errors have crept into the text of this play, which will be corrected when the title reprints. They are:

Page 7. The stage direction "Jane enters without the case" should read "with the case" in order for her to open it seven lines later.

Page 12. The direction "Mrs Murdoch exits L" should read "Mrs Murdoch enters L"

Page 28. After Marvo enters, coughing, the next line "There's a body on the floor ..." belongs to him and is not a continuation of Joy's speech

Page 29. Jane enters sleepily to say the line "What time is it?". This is not spoken by Serena.

Page 33. Joy's first line is said off stage. Line 15 should read "I suppose you're right. Monty told me he was listening to the radio ..."

20th October 2006